Essays on the Esoteric Tradition of Karma

By William Q. Judge Helena P. Blavatsky
and Annie Besant

Copyright © 2019 Lamp of Trismegistus. All rights reserved. No part of this publication may be reproduced or transmitted in any form or by any means, electronic or mechanical, including photocopying, recording, or by any information storage and retrieval system, without permission in writing from Lamp of Trismegistus. Reviewers may quote brief passages.

ISBN: 978-1-63118-426-0

Theosophical Classics

Other Books in this Series and Related Titles

Magical Essays and Instructions by Florence Farr (978-1-63118-418-5)

Plato and Platonism and Related Esoteric Essays
by Helena P. Blavatsky & others (978-1-63118-432-1)

The First and Second Gospels of the Infancy of Jesus Christ
by Thomas and James (978-1-63118-415-4)

Ancient Egyptian Mysteries and Hieroglyphics, Modern Freemasonry & Initiation of the Pyramid by various authors (978-1-63118-430-7)

Lost Atlantis and the Gods of Antiquity & Plato's History of Atlantis
by Carolus Kiesewetterus and Manly P. Hall (978-1-63118-431-4)

The Book of the Watchers by Enoch (978-1-63118-416-1)

The Smoky God or A Voyage to the Inner World
by Willis George Emerson (978-1-63118-423-9)

Rosa Alchemica, The Tables of Law & The Adoration of the Magi
by William Butler Yeats (978-1-63118-421-5)

A Collection of Fiction and Essays by Occult Writers on Supernatural, Metaphysical and Esoteric Subjects by various authors
(978-1-63118-712-4)

Occult Symbolism of Animals, Insects, Reptiles, Fish and Birds
by Manly P. Hall (978-1-63118-420-8)

The Feminine Occult by various authors (978-1-63118-711-7)

Thirty-One Hymns to the Star Goddess by Frater Achad
(978-1-63118-422-2)

Audio Versions are also Available on Audible and iTunes

Table of Contents

Introduction...7

Karma
by William Q. Judge...9

Aphorisms on Karma
by William Q. Judge...19

Karma in the Desatir
by William Q. Judge...25

Thoughts on Karma
by William Q. Judge...29

"Men Karmic Agents"
by William Q. Judge...37

Is Karma Only Punishment?
by William Q. Judge...41

Is Poverty Bad Karma?
by William Q. Judge...45

Thoughts on Karma and Reincarnation
by Helena P. Blavatsky...49

Karma-Nemesis
by Helena P. Blavatsky...63

Elementary Lessons on Karma
by Annie Besant...67

Introduction

The Theosophical movement of the late nineteenth century provided the world with an extensive canon of literature related to a wide variety of esoteric subjects. Theosophical publications were proliferous, producing thousands of articles on such subjects as mysticism, astral projection, Rosicrucianism, Greek philosophy, alchemy, Qabalah, Hinduism and Buddhism, Hermeticism and so on. Throughout this material, the unifying factor was always altruism and the concept of a Universal Brotherhood. Readers eagerly consumed these new ideas; however, with the passage of time, challenging world events, new pass-times and the ever-changing interests of our society, many of these works have fallen to the wayside and become nearly forgotten.

Lamp of Trismegistus is doing its part to help preserve humanity's spiritual history, by making some of these classics available to those students who are seeking to unearth the knowledge of these ancient colossi. As such, Lamp of Trismegistus offers its readers highlights of esoteric study, culled from a variety of authors and viewpoints, with the hope bringing education back into the forefront of our theosophical and spiritual lives. So, be sure to check out other titles in our *Theosophical Classics* collection as well as our *Foundations of Freemasonry Series*, *Esoteric Classics*, *Occult Fiction* and our *Christian Apocrypha Series*, and don't be afraid to let a little altruism into your own heart or even into your inner sanctum. You can also download the audio versions of most of these titles from iTunes or Audible for learning on the go.

Karma

By William Q. Judge

The child is the father of the man, and none the less true is it:

"My brothers! each mans life
The outcome of his former living is;
The bygone wrongs bring forth sorrows and woes
The bygone right breeds bliss.
This is the doctrine of Karma."

But in what way does this bygone wrong and right affect the present life? Is the stern nemesis ever following the weary traveler, with a calm, passionless, remorseless step? Is there no escape from its relentless hand? Does the eternal law of cause and effect, unmoved by sorrow and regret, ever deal out its measure of weal and woe as the consequence of past action? The shadow of the yesterday of sin--must it darken the life of today? Is Karma but another name for fate? Does the child unfold the page of the already written book of life in which each event is recorded without the possibility of escape? What is the relation of Karma to the life of the individual? Is there nothing for man to do but to weave the checkered wrap and woof of each earthly existence with the stained and discolored threads of past actions? Good resolves and evil tendencies sweep with resistless tide over the nature of man and we are told:

"Whatever action he performs, whether good or bad, everything done in a former body must necessarily be enjoyed or suffered."

There is good Karma, there is bad Karma, and as the wheel of life moves on, old Karma is exhausted and again fresh Karma is accumulated.

Although at first it may appear that nothing can be more fatalistic than this doctrine, yet a little consideration will show that in reality this is not the case. Karma is twofold, hidden and manifest, Karma is the man that is, Karma is his action. True that each action is a cause from which evolves the countless ramifications of effect in time and space.

"That which ye sow ye reap." In some sphere of action the harvest will be gathered. It is necessary that the man of action should realize this truth. It is equally necessary that the manifestations of this law in the operations of Karma should be clearly apprehended.

Karma, broadly speaking, may be said to be the continuance of the nature of the act, and each act contains within itself the past and future. Every defect which can be realized from an act must be implicit in the act itself or it could never come into existence. Effect is but the nature of the act and cannot exist distinct from its cause. Karma only produces the manifestation of that which already exists; being action it has its operation in time, and Karma may therefore be said to be the same action from another point of time. It must, moreover, be evident that not only is there a relation between the cause and the effect, but there must also be a relation between the cause and the individual who experiences the effect. If it were otherwise, any man would reap the effect of the actions of any other man. We may sometimes appear to reap the effects of the action of others, but this is only apparent. In point of fact it is our own action

*"...None else compels
None other holds you that ye live and die."*

It is therefore necessary in order to understand the nature of Karma and its relation to the individual to consider action in all its aspects. Every act proceeds from the mind. Beyond the mind there is no action and therefore no Karma. The basis of every act is desire. The plane of desire or egotism is itself action and the matrix of every act. This plane may be considered as non-manifest, yet having a dual manifestation in what we call cause and effect, that is, the act and its consequences. In reality, both the act and its consequences are the effect, the cause being on the plane of desire. Desire is therefore the basis of action in its first manifestation on the physical plane, and desire determines the continuation of the act in its karmic relation to the individual. For a man to be free from the effects of the Karma of any act he must have passed to a state no longer yielding a basis in which that act can inhere. The ripples in the water caused by the action of the stone will extend to the furthest limit of its expanse, but no further; they are bounded by the shore. Their course is ended when there is no longer a basis or suitable medium in which they can inhere; they expend their force and are not. Karma is, therefore, as dependent upon the present personality for its fulfillment, as it was upon the former for the first initial act. An illustration may be given which will help to explain this.

A seed, say for instance mustard, will produce a mustard tree and nothing else; but in order that it should be produced, it is necessary that the cooperation of soil and culture should be equally present. Without the seed, however much the ground may be tilled and watered, it will not bring forth the plant, but the seed is equally inoperative without the joint action of the soil and culture.

The first great result of Karmic action is the incarnation in physical life. The birth-seeking entity consisting of desires and tendencies, presses forward towards incarnation. It is governed in the selection of its scene of manifestation by the law of economy. Whatever is the ruling tendency, that is to say, whatever group of affinities is strongest, those affinities will lead it to the point of manifestation at which there is the least opposition. It incarnates in those surroundings most in harmony with its Karmic tendencies and all the effects of actions contained in the Karma so manifesting will be experienced by the individual. This governs the station of life, the sex, the conditions of the irresponsible years of childhood, the constitution with the various diseases inherent in it, and in fact all those determining forces of physical existence which are ordinarily classed under the terms, "heredity," and "national characteristics."

It is really the law of economy which is the truth underlying these terms and which explains them. Take for instance a nation with certain special characteristics. These are the plane of expansion for any entity whose greatest number of affinities are in harmony with those characteristics. The incoming entity following the law of least resistance becomes incarnated in that nation, and all Karmic effects following such characteristics will accrue to the individual. This will explain what is the meaning of such expressions as the "Karma of nations," and what is true of the nation will also apply to family and caste.

It must, however, be remembered that there are many tendencies which are not exhausted in the act of incarnation. It may happen that the Karma which caused an entity to incarnate in any particular surrounding, was only strong enough to carry it into physical existence. Being exhausted in that direction, freedom is obtained for the manifestation of other tendencies and their Karmic effects. For instance, Karmic force may cause an entity to incarnate in a humble sphere of life. He may be born as the child of poor parents. The Karma follows the entity, endures for a longer or shorter time, and becomes exhausted. From that point, the child takes a line of life totally different from his surroundings. Other affinities engendered by former action express themselves in their Karmic results. The lingering effect of the past Karma may still manifest itself in the way of obstacles and obstructions, which are surmounted with varying degrees of success according to their intensity.

From the standpoint of a special creation for each entity entering the world, there is vast and unaccountable injustice. From the standpoint of Karma, the strange vicissitudes and apparent chances of life can be considered in a different light as the unerring manifestation of cause and sequence. In a family under the same conditions of poverty and ignorance, one child will be separated from the others and thrown into surroundings very dissimilar. He may be adopted by a rich man, or through some freak of fortune receive an education giving him at once a different position. The Karma of incarnation being exhausted, other Karma asserts itself.

A very important question is here presented: Can an individual affect his own Karma, and if so to what degree and in what manner?

It has been said that Karma is the continuance of the act, and for any particular line of Karma to exert itself it is necessary that there should be the basis of the act engendering that Karma in which it can adhere and operate. But action has many planes in which it can inhere. There is the physical plane, the body with its senses and organs; then there is the intellectual plane, memory, which binds the impressions of the senses into a consecutive whole and reason puts in orderly arrangement its storehouse of facts. Beyond the plane of intellect there is the plane of emotion, the plane of preference for one object rather than another: the fourth principle of the man. These three, physical, intellectual, and emotional, deal entirely with objects of sense perception and may be called the great battlefield of Karma. There is also the plane of ethics, the plane of discrimination of the "I ought to do this, I ought not to do that." This plane harmonizes the intellect and the emotions. All these are the planes of Karma or action: what to do, and what not to do. It is the mind as the basis of desire that initiates action on the various planes, and it is only through the mind that the effects of rest and action can be received.

An entity enters incarnation with Karmic energy from past existences, that is to say the action of past lives is awaiting its development as effect. This Karmic energy presses into manifestation in harmony with the basic nature of the act. Physical Karma will manifest in the physical tendencies bringing enjoyment and suffering. The intellectual and the ethical planes are also in the same manner the result of the past Karmic tendencies and the man as he is, with his moral and intellectual faculties, is in unbroken continuity with the past.

The entity at birth has therefore a definite amount of Karmic energy. After incarnation this awaits the period in life at which fresh Karma begins. Up to the time of responsibility it is as we have seen the initial Karma only that manifests. From that time the fresh personality becomes the ruler of his own destiny. It is a great mistake to suppose that an individual is the mere puppet of the past, the helpless victim of fate. The law of Karma is not fatalism, and a little consideration will show that it is possible for an individual to affect his own Karma. If a greater amount of energy be taken up on one plane than on another this will cause the past Karma to unfold itself on that plane. For instance, one who lives entirely on the plane of sense gratification will from the plane beyond draw the energy required for the fulfillment of his desires. Let us illustrate by dividing man into upper and lower nature. By directing the mind and aspirations to the lower plane, a "fire" or center of attraction, is set up there, and in order to feed and fatten it, the energies of the whole upper plane are drawn down and exhausted in supplying the need of energy which exists below due to the indulgence of sense gratification. On the other hand, the center of attraction may be fixed in the upper portion, and then all the needed energy goes there to result in increase of spirituality. It must be remembered that Nature is all bountiful and withholds not her hand. The demand is made, and the supply will come. But at what cost? That energy which should have strengthened the moral nature and fulfilled the aspirations after good, is drawn to the lower desires. By degrees the higher planes are exhausted of vitality and the good and bad Karma of an entity will be absorbed on the physical plane. If on the other hand the interest is detached from the plane of sense gratification, if there is a constant effort to fix the mind on the attainment of the highest ideal, the result will be that the past Karma will find no basis in which to inhere on the physical plane. Karma will therefore be manifested only in harmony with the plane of desire. The sense energy of the physical plane will exhaust itself on a higher plane and thus become transmuted in its effects.

What are the means through which the effects of Karma can be thus changed, is also clear. A person can have no attachment for a thing he does not think about, therefore the first step must be to fix the thought on the highest ideal. In this connection one remark may be made on the subject of repentance. Repentance is a form of thought in which the mind is constantly recurring to a sin. It has therefore to be avoided if one would set the mind free from sin and its Karmic results. All sin has its origin in the mind. The more the mind dwells on any course of conduct, whether with pleasure or pain, the less chance is there for it to become detached from such action. The *manas* (mind) is the knot of the heart, when that is untied from any object, in other words when the mind loses its interest in any object, there will no longer be a link between the Karma connected with that object and the individual.

It is the attitude of the mind which draws the Karmic cords tightly around the soul. It imprisons the aspirations and binds them with chains of difficulty and obstruction. It is desire that causes the past Karma to take form and shape and build the house of clay. It must be through non-attachment that the soul will burst through the walls of pain, it will be only through a change of mind that the Karmic burden will be lifted.

It will appear, therefore, that although absolutely true that action brings its own result, "there is no destruction here of actions good or not good. Coming to one body after another they become ripened in their respective ways." Yet this ripening is the act of the individual. Free will of man asserts itself and he becomes his own savior. To the worldly man Karma is a stern Nemesis, to the spiritual man Karma unfolds itself in harmony with his highest aspirations. He will look with tranquility alike on past and future, neither dwelling with remorse on past sin nor living in expectation of reward for present action.

Aphorisms on Karma

By William Q. Judge

(1) There is no Karma unless there is a being to make it or feel its effects.

(2) Karma is the adjustment of effects flowing from causes, during which the being upon whom and through whom that adjustment is effected experiences pain or pleasure.

(3) Karma is an undeviating and unerring tendency in the Universe to restore equilibrium, and it operates incessantly.

(4) The apparent stoppage of this restoration to equilibrium is due to the necessary adjustment of disturbance at some other spot, place, or focus which is visible only to the Yogi, to the Sage, or the perfect Seer: there is therefore no stoppage, but only a hiding from view.

(5) Karma operates on all things and beings from the minutest conceivable atom to Brahma. Proceeding in the three worlds men, gods, and the elemental beings, no spot in the manifested universe is exempt from its sway.

(6) Karma is not subject to time, and therefore he who knows what is the ultimate division of time in this Universe knows Karma.

(7) For all other men Karma is in its essential nature unknown and unknowable.

(8) But its action may be known by calculation from cause to effect; and this calculation is possible because the effect is wrapped up in and is not succeedent to the cause.

(9) The Karma of this earth is the combination of the acts and thoughts of all beings of every grade which were concerned in the preceding Manvantara or evolutionary stream from which ours flows.

(10) And as those beings include Lords of Power and Holy Men, as well as weak and wicked ones, the period of the earth's duration is greater than that of any entity or race upon it.

(11) Because the Karma of this earth and its races began in a past too far back for human minds to reach, an inquiry into its beginning is useless and profitless.

(12) Karmic causes already set in motion must be allowed to sweep on until exhausted, but this permits no man to refuse to help his fellows and every sentient being.

(13) The effects may be counteracted or mitigated by the thoughts and acts of oneself or of another, and then the resulting effects represent the combination and interaction of the whole number of causes

involved in producing the effects.

(14) In the life of worlds, races, nations, and individuals, Karma cannot act unless there is an appropriate instrument provided for its action.

(15) And until such appropriate instrument is found, that Karma related to it remains unexpended.

(16) While a man is experiencing Karma in the instrument provided, his other unexpended Karma is not exhausted through other beings or means, but is held reserved for future operation; and lapse of time during which no operation of that Karma is felt causes no deterioration in its force or change in its nature.

(17) The appropriateness of an instrument for the operation of Karma consists in the exact connection and relation of the Karma with the body, mind, intellectual and psychical nature acquired for use by the Ego in any life.

(18) Every instrument used by any Ego in any life is appropriate to the Karma operating through it.

(19) Changes may occur in the instrument during one life so as to make it appropriate for a new class of Karma, and this may take place in two ways: (a) through intensity of thought and the power of a vow, and (b) through natural alterations due to complete exhaustion of old causes.

(20) As body and mind and soul have each a

power of independent action, any one of these may exhaust, independently of the others, some Karmic causes more remote from or nearer to the time of their inception than those operating through other channels.

(21) Karma is both merciful and just. Mercy and Justice are only opposite poles of a single whole; and Mercy without Justice is not possible in the operations of Karma. That which man calls Mercy and Justice is defective, errant, and impure.

(22) Karma may be of three sorts: (a) presently operative in this life through the appropriate instruments; (b) that which is being made or stored up to be exhausted in the future; Karma held over from past life or lives and not operating yet because inhibited by inappropriateness of the instrument in use by the Ego, or by the force of Karma now operating.

(23) Three fields of operation are used in each being by Karma: (a) the body and the circumstances; (b) the mind and intellect; the psychic and astral planes.

(24) Held-over Karma or present Karma may each, or both at once, operate in all of the three fields of Karmic operation at once, or in either of those fields a different class of Karma from that using the others may operate at the same time.

(25) Birth into any sort of body and to obtain the fruits of any sort of Karma is due to the preponderance of the line of Karmic tendency.

(26) The sway of Karmic tendency will influence the incarnation of an Ego, or any family of Egos, for three lives at least, when measures of repression, elimination, or counteraction are not adopted.

(27) Measures taken by an Ego to repress tendency, eliminate defects, and to counteract by setting up different causes, will alter the sway of Karmic tendency and shorten its influence in accordance with the strength or weakness of the efforts expended in carrying out the measures adopted.

(28) No man but a sage or true seer can judge another's Karma. Hence while each receives his deserts, appearances may

deceive, and birth into Poverty or heavy trial may not be punishment for bad Karma, for Egos continually incarnate into poor surroundings where they experience difficulties and trials which are for the discipline of the Ego and result in strength, fortitude, and sympathy.

(29) Race-Karma influences each unit in the race through the law of Distribution. National Karma operates on the members of the nation by the same law more concentrated. Family Karma governs only with a nation where families have been kept pure and distinct; for in any nation where there is a mixture of

family - as obtains in each Kaliyuga period - family Karma is in general distributed over a nation. But even at such periods some families remain coherent for long periods, and then the members feel the sway of family Karma. The word "family" may include several smaller families.

(30) Karma operates to produce cataclysms of nature by concatenation through the mental and astral planes of being. A cataclysm may be traced to an immediate physical cause such as internal fire and atmospheric disturbance, but these have been brought on by the disturbance created through the dynamic power of human thought.

(31) Egos who have no Karmic connection with a portion of the globe where a cataclysm is coming on are kept without the latter's operation in two ways: (*a*) by repulsion acting on their inner nature, and (*b*) by being called and warned by those who watch the progress of the world.

Karma in the Desatir

By William Q. Judge

The *Desatir* is a collection of the writings of the different Persian Prophets, one of whom was Zoroaster. The last was alive in the time of Khusro Parvez, who was contemporary with the Emperor Revaclius and died only nine years before the end of the ancient Persian monarchy. Sir William Jones was the first who drew the attention of European scholars to the *Desatir*. It is divided into books of the different prophets. In this article the selections are from the "*Prophet Abad.*"

"In the name of Lareng! Mezdam separated man from the other animals by the distinction of a soul, which is a free and independent substance, without a body or anything material, indivisible and without position, by which he attaineth to the glory of the angels.

"By his knowledge he united the soul with the elemental body. If one doeth good in an elemental body, and possesseth useful knowledge, and acts aright, and is a Hirtasp, and doth not give pain to harmless animals; when he putteth off the inferior body I will introduce him to the abode of the angels that he may see me with the nearest angels.

"And every one who wisheth to return to the lower world and is a doer of good shall, according to his knowledge and conversation and actions, receive something, either as a King or Prime Minister, or some high office or wealth, until he meeteth with a reward suited to his deeds.

> "Those who, in the season of prosperity, experience pain and grief suffer them on account of their words or deeds in a former body, for which the Most Just now punisheth them.
>
> "In the name of Lareng! Whosoever is an evil doer, on him He first inflicteth pain under human form: for sickness, sufferings of children while in their mothers womb, and after they are out of it, and suicide, and being hurt by ravenous animals, and death, and being subjected to want from birth to death, are all retributions for past actions: and in like manner as to goodness.
>
> "If anyone knowingly and intentionally kill a harmless animal and do not meet with retribution in the same life either from the unseen or the earthly ruler, he will find punishment awaiting him at his next coming."

Certain verses declare that foolish and evildoers are condemned to the bodies of vegetables, and the very wicked to the form of minerals, and then declare they so remain,

> "Until their sins be purified, after which they are delivered from this suffering and are once more united to a human body: and according as they act in it they again meet with retribution."

In the *Desatir* the doctrine is held that animals are also subject to punishment by retributive Karma; thus:

> "If a ravenous animal kill a harmless animal it must be regarded as retaliation on the slain, since ferocious animals exist for the purpose of inflicting such punishment. The slaying of ravenous animals is laudable, since they in a former existence have been shedders of blood and slew the guiltless. The punisher of such is blest.

"The lion, the tiger, the leopard, the panther, and the wolf, with all ravenous animals, whether birds, quadrupeds, or creeping things, have once possessed authority; and everyone whom they kill hath been their aider or abettor who did evil by supporting or assisting, or by the orders of, that exalted class; and having given pain to harmless animals are now punished by their own masters. In fine, these grandees, being invested with the forms of ravenous beasts, expire of suffering and wounds according to their misdeeds; and if any guilt remain they will return a second time and suffer punishment along with their accomplices."

Thoughts on Karma

By William W. Judge

Every day in life we see people overtaken by circumstances either good or bad and coming in blocks all at once or scattered over long periods of time. Some are for a whole life in a miserable condition, and others for many years the very reverse; while still others are miserable or happy by snatches. I speak, of course, of the circumstances of life irrespective of the effect on the mind of the person, for it may often be that a man is not unhappy under adverse circumstances, and some are able to extract good from the very strait lines they are put within. Now all this is the Karma of those who are the experiencers, and therefore we ask ourselves if Karma may fall in a lump or may be strung out over a long space of years. And the question is also asked if the circumstances of this life are the sum total result of the life, which has immediately preceded it.

There is a little story told to a German mystic in this century by an old man, another mystic, when asked the meaning of the verse in the Bible which says that the sins of the father will be visited on the children to the third and fourth generation. He said: "There was once an Eastern king who had one son, and this son committed a deed the penalty of which was that he should be killed by a great stone thrown upon him. But as it was seen that this would not repair the wrong nor give to the offender the chance to become a better man, the counselors of the king advised that the stone should be broken into small pieces, and those be thrown at the son, and at his children and grandchildren, as they were able to bear it. It was so done, and all were in some sense sufferers yet none were destroyed." It was argued, of course, in this case that the children and grandchildren could not have been born in the family of the prince if they had not had some hand in the past, in other lives, in the formation of his character, and for that reason they should share to some extent in his punishment. In no other way than this can the Christian verses be understood if we are to attribute justice to the God of the Christians.

Each Ego is attracted to the body in which he will meet his just deserts, but also for another reason. That is, that not only is the body to give opportunity for his just reward or punishment, but also for that he in the past was connected with the family in which the body was born, and the stream of heredity to which it belongs is his too. It is therefore a question not alone of desert and similarity, but one of responsibility. Justice orders that the Ego shall suffer or enjoy irrespective of what family he comes to; similarity decrees that he shall come to the family in which there is some characteristic similar to one or many of his and thus having a drawing power; but responsibility, which is compounded of justice, directs that the Ego shall come to the race or the nation or the family to which its responsibility lies for the part taken by it in other lives in forming of the general character, or affecting that physical stream of heredity that has so much influence on those who are involved in it. Therefore it is just that even the grandchildren shall suffer if they in the past have had a hand in molding the family or even in bringing about a social order that is detrimental to those who fall into it through incarnation. I use the word responsibility to indicate something composed of similarity and justice. It may be described by other words probably quite as well, and in the present state of the English language very likely will be. An Ego may have no direct responsibility for a family, national, or race condition, and yet be drawn into incarnation there. In such an event it is similarity of character, which causes the place of rebirth, for the being coming to the abode of mortals is drawn like electricity along the path of least resistance and of greatest conductibility. But where the reincarnating Ego is directly responsible for family or race conditions, it will decide itself, upon exact principles of justice and in order to meet its obligations, to be reborn where it shall receive, as grandchild if you will, physically or otherwise the results of its former acts. This decision is made at the emergence from Devachan. It is thus entirely just, no matter whether the new physical brain is able or not to pick up the lost threads of memory.

So today, in our civilization, we are all under the penalty of our forefathers sins, living in bodies which medical science has shown are sown with diseases of brain and flesh and blood coming in the turbid stream of heredity through the centuries. These disturbances were brought about by ourselves in other centuries, in ignorance, perhaps, of consequences so far-reaching, but that ignorance lessens only the higher moral responsibility and tends to confine the results to physical suffering. This can very well lead, as it often does, to efforts on the part of many reincarnating Egos in the direction of general reform.

It was through a belief in this that the ancients attempted to form and keep up in India a pure family stream such as the highest caste of Brahmin. For they knew that if such a clean family line could be kept existing for many centuries, it would develop the power of repelling Egos on the way to rebirth if they were not in character up to the standard of that stream of life. Thus only teachers by nature, of high moral and spiritual elevation, would come upon the scene to act as regenerators and saviors for all other classes. But under the iron rule of cyclic law this degenerated in time, leaving now only an imitation of the real thing.

A variation of the Eastern story told above is that the advice of the king's counselors was that the broken stone should be cast at the prince. This was done, and the result was that he was not killed but suffered while the pieces were being thrown. It gives another Karmic law, that is, that a given amount of force of a Karmic character may be thrown at one or fall upon one at once, in bulk, so to say, or may be divided up into smaller pieces, the sum of which represents the whole mass of Karmic force. And so we see it in life. Men suffer through many years an amount of adverse Karma, which, if it were to fall all at once, would crush them. Others for a long time have general good fortune that might unseat the reason if experienced in one day; and the latter happens also, for we know of those who have been destroyed by the sudden coming of what is called great good fortune.

This law is seen also in physics. A piece of glass may be broken at once by a single blow, or the same amount of force put into a number of taps continuously repeated will accomplish the same result and mash the glass. And with the emotions we observe the same law followed by even the most ignorant, for we do not tell bad news at once to the person who is the sufferer, but get at it slowly by degrees; and often when disaster is suddenly heard of, the person who hears it is prostrated. In both cases the sorrow caused is the same, but the method of imparting the news differs. Indeed, in whatever direction we look, this law is observed to work. It is universal, and it ought to be applied to Karma as well as to anything else.

Whether the life we are now living is the net result of the one just preceding is answered by Patanjali in his 8th and 9th aphorisms, Book IV.

"From these works there results, in every incarnation, a manifestation of only those mental deposits which can come to fructification in the environment provided. Although the manifestation of mental deposits may be intercepted by unsuitable environments, differing as to class, place, and time, there is an immediate relation between them, because the memory and the train of self- reproductive thoughts are identical," and also by other doctrines of the ancients. When a body is taken up, only that sort of Karma which can operate through it will make itself felt. This is what Patanjali means. The "environment" is the body, with the mind, the plastic nature, and the emotions and desires. Hence one may have been great or the reverse in the preceding life, and now have only the environment which will serve for the exhaustion of some Karma left over from lives many incarnations distant. This unexhausted Karma is known as stored-up Karma. It may or may not come into operation now, and it can also be brought out into view by violent effort of the mind leading to such changes as to alter the bodily

apparatus and make it equivalent to a new body. But as the majority of men are lazy of mind and nature, they suffer themselves to run with the great family or national stream, and so through one life make no changes of this inner nature. Karma in their cases operates through what Patanjali calls "mental deposits." These are the net results stored from each life by *Manas*. For as body dies, taking brain with it, there can be no storage there nor means of connecting with the next earth-life; the division known as *Kama* is dissipated or purged away together with astral body at some time before rebirth; astral body retains nothing--as a general rule for the new life, and the value or summation of those skandhas which belong to *Kama* is concentrated and deposited in *Manas* or the mind. So, when the immortal being returns, he is really *Manas-Buddhi-Atma* seeking a new environment, which is found in a new body, *prana, Kama,* and astral double. Hence, and because under the sway of cyclic law, the reincarnation can only furnish an engine of a horsepower, so to say, which is very much lower than the potential energies stored in *Manas,* and thus there remain unexhausted "mental deposits," or unexhausted Karma. The Ego may therefore be expending a certain line of Karma, always bringing it to similar environments until that class of Karma shall be so exhausted or weakened as to permit another set of "mental deposits" to preponderate, whereupon the next incarnation will be in a different environment which shall give opportunity for the new set of deposits to bring about new or different Karma.

The object that is indicated for life by all this is, to so live and think during each life as to generate no new Karma, or cause for bondage, while one is working off the stock in hand, in order that on closing each life-account one shall have wiped off so much as that permits. The old "mental deposits" will thus gradually move up into action and exhaustion from life to life, at last leaving the man in a condition where he can master all and step into true consciousness, prepared to renounce final reward in order that he may remain with humanity, making no new Karma himself and helping others along the steep road to perfection.

"Men Karmic Agents"
By William Q. Judge

The above is the title of an essay in the T.P.S. series by Alexander Fullerton, in which he treats the question solely in regard to whether we should take punitive or reformatory measures with those of our fellow-beings who transgress in those respects in which we so often see culpability. In that essay he has said a great deal that cannot be controverted from the general rules prevailing, but there are other considerations, and also other ways of understanding the term "Karmic Agent."

For this Madame Blavatsky had a particular and technical meaning under which the Karmic Agent is at once removed from the ordinary general mass to which the essay in the *Siftings* has reference. A statement of the law of Karma of course makes not only men karmic agents but also every other being in the Cosmos, inasmuch as they are all under the law of action and reaction, and, with the same law, go to make Cosmos what it is. Taken as a unit in the general mass of men, each man is a Karmic agent in the above sense, just as each horse and dog, or the rain and the sun are. So in our daily actions, even the smallest, whether we are conscious or not of the effect, we are such agents. A single word of ours may have an influence for a lifetime upon another. It may cause once more the fire of passion to blaze up, or bring about a great change for good. We may be the means of another's being late for an appointment and thus save him from calamity or the reverse, and so on infinitely. But all this is very different from the technical sense I have referred to, and which might be taken to be the sense of the title of the article thus specially removed from the general class.

The special sense is in this: a "Karmic Agent" is one who concentrates more rapidly than is usual the lines of influence that bring about events sometimes in a strange and subtle way. Of these there are two classes; the first, those among the mass who, from the lives they have led in the past, arrive in this one gifted--or cursed with the power unknown to themselves. The second, those who by training have the power, or rather have become concentrators of the forces, and know it to be the case. Of these are the Adepts, both great and small. An instance of this may be found in the life of Zanoni as related by Bulwer Lytton. It was observed that those who met Zanoni soon showed in their affairs very great changes, and although Lytton's son has said, out of his imagination, I think, that his father never intended what theosophists say he did by the book, there is no doubt that Bulwer meant to teach and illustrate the law.

In Patanjali's *Yoga Aphorisms* it is also spoken of in the 36th Aphorism, second book, thus (*Amer. Ed.*): "When veracity is complete the Yogi becomes the focus for the Karma resulting from all works, good and bad"; and in the Bombay edition, "when veracity is complete he is the receptacle of the fruit of works."

It is a well-known tradition in India, called by the civilized West a superstition, that if one should meet and talk with an Adept his Karma good and bad would come to a head more quickly than usual, and thus that the Adept could confer a boon, letting the evil pass and increasing the good. I have conversed with those who asserted they had by chance met Yogis in the forest with whom they talked, telling them that some dear friend was sick unto death, and then on returning home found that the sickness had all gone at the very time of the conversation. And others met such men, who told them that the meeting would bring on the opposite by reason of quick concentration, but that even that would be a benefit, as it would, as it were, eat up much unpleasant Karma once for all. Of this class of traditions is the story of the centurion's daughter and Jesus of Nazareth.

And H.P.B. held that there are many people in the world, engaged in its affairs, who are, without knowing it, Karmic agents in this special sense, and continually bring to others good and bad sudden effects which otherwise would have come slowly to pass, spread over many more days or years, and showing in a number of small events instead of in one.

If this theory be true, we have here also the explanation of the superstition of the evil eye, which is only a corrupt form of the knowledge that there are such Karmic agents among us who by looking at others draw together very quickly effects that without the presence of the Karmic agent might never have been noticed because of their taking more time to transpire.

But if we follow too strictly the theory that men are Karmic agents for the punishment or reformation of others, many mistakes will be made and much bad feeling engendered in others, making it inevitable that we who cause these feelings must receive some day, in this life or another, the exact reaction. And on the other hand, we should not shrink from the duty to relieve pain and sorrow if we can, for it is both cowardice and conceit to say that we will not help this or that man because it is his Karma to suffer. In the face of suffering it is our good Karma to relieve it if in our power. We are ignorant at best, and cannot tell what will be the next result of what we are about to do or to suggest; hence it is wiser not to assume too often and on too small occasions to be the reformers or punishers as agents for Karma of those who seem to offend.

Is Karma Only Punishment?

By William Q. Judge

The following query has been received from H.M.H.: "In August PATH Hadji Erinn, in reply to the above question, stated that 'those who have wealth, and the happy mother seeing all her children respected and virtuous, are favorites of Karma. I and others believe that these apparent favors are only punishment or obstacles, and others think that the terms *punishment* and *reward* should not be used."

I cannot agree with this view, nor with the suggestion that punishment and reward should not be used as terms. It is easy to reduce everything to a primordial basis when one may say that all is the absolute. But such is only the method of those who *affirm* and *deny*. They say there is no evil, there is no death; all is good, all is life. In this way we are reduced to absurdities, inasmuch as we then have no terms to designate very evident things and conditions. As well say there is no *gold* and no *iron*, because both are equally *matter*. While we continue to be human beings we must use terms that shall express our conscious perception of ideas and things.

It is therefore quite proper to say that an unhappy or miserably circumstanced person is undergoing punishment, and that the wealthy or happy person is having reward. Otherwise there is no sense in our doctrine.

The misunderstanding shown in the question is due to inaccurate thinking upon the subject of Karma. One branch of this law deals with the vicissitudes of life, with the differing states of men. One man has opportunity and happiness, another meets only the opposite. Why is this? It is because each state is the exact result bound to come from his having disturbed or preserved the harmony of nature. The person given wealth in this life is he who in the preceding incarnation suffered from its absence or had been deprived of it unjustly. What are we to call it but reward? If we say *compensation,* we express exactly the same idea. And we cannot get the world to adopt verbosity in speech so as to say, "All this is due to that man's having preserved the cosmic harmony."

The point really in the questioners mind is, in fact, quite different from the one expressed; he has mistaken one for the other; he is thinking of the fact so frequently obtruded before us that the man who has the opportunity of wealth or power oft misuses it and becomes selfish or tyrannous. But this does not alter the conclusion that he is having his reward. Karma will take care of him; and if he does not use the opportunity for the good of his fellows, or if he does evil to them, he will have punishment upon coming back again to earth. It is true enough, as Jesus said, that "it is difficult for the rich man to enter heaven," but there are other possessions of the man besides wealth that constitute greater obstacles to development, and they are punishments and may coexist in the life of one man with the reward of wealth or the like. I mean the obstruction and hindrance found in stupidity, or natural baseness, or in physical sensual tendencies. These are more likely to keep him from progress and ultimate salvation than all the wealth or good luck that any one person ever enjoyed.

In such cases--and they are not a few--we see Karmic reward upon the outer material plane in the wealth and propitious arrangement of life, and on the inner character the punishment of being unable or unfit through many defects of mind or nature. This picture can be reversed with equal propriety. I doubt if the questioner has devoted his mind to analyzing the subject in this manner.

Every man, however, is endowed with conscience and the power to use his life, whatever its form or circumstance, in the proper way, so as to extract from it all the good for himself and his fellows that his limitations of character will permit. It is his duty so to do, and as he neglects or obeys, so will be his subsequent *punishment* or *reward*.

There may also be another sort of wealth than mere gold, another sort of power than position in politics or society. The powerful, wide, all-embracing, rapidly-acting brain stored with knowledge is a vast possession which one man may enjoy. He can use it properly or improperly. It may lead him to excesses, to vileness, to the very opposite of all that is good. It is his reward for a long past life of stupidity followed by others of noble deeds and thoughts. What will the questioner do with this? The possessor thus given a reward may misuse it so as to turn it, next time he is born, into a source of punishment. We are thus continually fitting our arrows to the bow, drawing them back hard to the ear, and shooting them forth from us. When we enter the field of earth-life again, they will surely strike us or our enemies of human shape or the circumstances which otherwise would hurt us. It is not the arrow or the bow that counts, but the motive and the thought with which the missile is shot.

Is Poverty Bad Karma?

By William Q. Judge

The question of what is good Karma and what is bad, has been usually considered by theosophists, from a very worldly and selfish standpoint. The commercial element has entered into the calculation as to the result of merit and demerit. Eternal Justice, which is but another name for Karma, has been spoken of as awarding this or that state of life to the reincarnating ego solely as a mere balance of accounts in a ledger, with a payment in one case by way of reward and a judgment for debt in another by way of punishment.

It has been often thought that if a man be rich and well circumstanced it must follow that in his prior incarnation he was good although poor; and that if he now be in poverty the conclusion is that, when on earth before, his life was bad if rich. So it has come about that the sole test of good or bad Karma is one founded entirely upon his purse. But is poverty with all its miseries bad Karma? Does it follow, because a man is born in the lowest station in life, compelled always to live in the humblest way, often starving and hearing his wife and children cry out for food, that therefore he is suffering from bad Karma?

If we look at the question entirely from the plane of this one life, this personality, then of course what is disagreeable and painful in life may be said to be bad. But if we regard all conditions of life as experiences undergone by the ego for the purpose of development, then even poverty ceases to be "bad

Karma." Strength comes only through trial and exercise. In poverty are some of the greatest tests for endurance, the best means for developing the strength of character which alone leads to greatness. These egos, then, whom we perceive around us encased in bodies whose environment is so harsh that endurance is needed to sustain the struggle, are voluntarily, for all we know, going through that difficult school so as to acquire further deep experience and with it strength.

The old definition of what is good and what bad Karma is the best. That is: "Good Karma is that which is pleasing to Ishvara, and bad that which is displeasing to Ishvara." There is here but very little room for dispute as to poverty or wealth; for the test and measure are not according to our present evanescent human tastes and desires, but are removed to the judgment of the immortal self-- Ishvara. The self may not wish for the pleasures of wealth, but seeing the necessity for discipline decides to assume life among mortals in that low station where endurance, patience, and strength may be acquired by experience. There is no other way to implant in the character the lessons of life.

It may then be asked if all poverty and low condition are good Karma? This we can answer, under the rule laid down, in the negative. Some such lives, indeed many of them, are bad Karma, displeasing to the immortal self imprisoned in the body, because they are not by deliberate choice, but the result of causes blindly set in motion in previous lives, sure to result in planting within the person the seeds of wickedness that must later be uprooted with painful effort. Under this canon, then, we would say that the masses of poor people who are not bad in nature are enduring oftener than not good Karma, because it is in the line of experience Ishvara has chosen, and that only those poor people who are wicked can be said to be suffering bad Karma, because they are doing and making that which is displeasing to the immortal self within.

Thoughts on Karma and Reincarnation

By Helena P. Blavatsky

"In man there are arteries, thin as a hair split 1,000 times, filled with fluids blue, red, green, yellow, etc. The tenuous involucrum (the base or ethereal frame of the astral body) is lodged in them, and the ideal residues of the experiences of the former embodiments (or incarnations) adhere to the said tenuous involucrum, and accompany it in its passage from body to body."
—UPANISHADS.

"Judge of a man by his questions rather than by his answers," teaches the wily Voltaire. The advice stops halfway in our case. To become complete and cover the whole ground, we have to add, "ascertain the motive which prompts the questioner." A man may offer a query from a sincere impulse to learn and to know. Another person will ask eternal questions, with no better motive than a desire of cavilling and proving his adversary in the wrong.

Not a few among the "inquirers into Theosophy," as they introduce themselves, belong to this latter category. We have found in it Materialists and Spiritualists, Agnostics and Christians. Some of them, though rarely, are "open to conviction"—as they say; others, thinking with Cicero that no liberal, truth-seeking man should ever impute a charge of unsteadiness to anyone for having changed his opinions—become really converted and join our ranks. But there are those also—and these form the majority—who, while representing themselves as inquirers, are in truth carpers. Whether owing to narrowness of mind or foolhardiness they intrench themselves behind their own preconceived and not unseldom shallow beliefs and opinions, and will not budge from them. Such a "seeker" is hopeless, as his desire to investigate the truth is a pretext, not even a fearless mask, but simply a false nose. He has neither the open determination of an avowed materialists, nor the serene coolness of a "Sir Oracle." But—

> *". . . you may as well*
> *Forbid the sea for to obey the moon*
> *As or by oath remove, or counsel shake,*
> *The fabric of his folly . . ."*

Therefore, a "seeker after truth" of this kind had better be severely left alone. He is intractable, because he is either a skin-deep sciolist, a self-opinionated theorist or a fool. As a general rule, he talks reincarnation before he has even learned the difference between metempsychosis, which is the transmigration of the human Soul into an animal form, and Reincarnation, or the rebirth of the same Ego in successive human bodies. Ignorant of the true meaning of the Greek word, he does not even suspect how absurd, in philosophy, is this purely exoteric doctrine of transmigrations into animals. Useless to tell him that Nature, propelled by Karma, never recedes, but strives ever forward in her work on the physical plane; that she may lodge a human soul in the body of a man, morally ten times lower than any animal, but she will not reverse the order of her kingdoms; and while leading the irrational monad of a beast of a higher order into the human form at the first hour of a Manvantara, she will not guide that Ego, once it has become a man, even of the lowest kind, back into the animal species—not during that cycle (or Kalpa) at any rate.

The list of queer "investigators" is by no means exhausted with these amiable seekers. There are two other classes—Christians and Spiritualists, the latter being in some respects, more formidable than any. The former having been born and bred believers in the Bible and supernatural "miracles" on authority, or "thirty-seventh hand evidence," to use a popular proverb, are often forced to yield in the face of the firsthand testimony of their own reason and senses; and then they are amenable to reason and conviction. They had formed a priori opinions and got crystallized in them as a fly in a piece of amber. But that amber has cracked, and, as one of the signs of the times, they have bethought themselves of a somewhat tardy still sincere search, to either justify their early opinions, or else part company with them for good. Having found out that their religion—like that of the great majority of their fellow men—had been founded on human not divine respect, they come to us as they would to surgical operators, believing that theosophists can remove all the old cobwebs from their bewildered brains. Sometimes it does so happen; once made to see the fallacy of first accepting and identifying themselves with any form of belief, and then only seeking, years later, for reasons to justify it, they very naturally try to avoid falling again into the same mistake. They had once to content themselves with such interpretations of their time-honoured dogmas as the fallacy and often the absurdity of the latter would afford; but now, they seek to learn and understand before they believe.

This is the right and purely theosophical state of mind, and is quite consistent with the precept of Lord Buddha, who taught never to believe merely on authority but to test the latter by means of our personal reason and highest intuition. It is only such seekers after the eternal truth who can profit by the lessons of old Eastern Wisdom.

It is our duty, therefore, to help them to defend their new ideals by furnishing them with the most adequate and far-reaching weapons. For they will have to encounter, not only Materialists and Spiritualists, but also to break a lance with their ex-coreligionists. These will bring to bear upon them the whole of their arsenal, composed of the popguns of biblical casuistry and interpretations based on the dead-letter texts and the disingenuous translation of pseudo revelation. They have to be prepared. They will be told, for instance, that there is not a word in the Bible which would warrant belief in reincarnation, or life, more than once, on this earth. Biologists and physiologists will laugh at such a theory, and assure them that it is opposed by the fact that no man has a glimpse of recollection of any past life. Shallow metaphysicians, and supporters of the easy-going Church ethics of this age, will gravely maintain the injustice there would be in a posterior punishment, in the present life, for deeds committed in a previous existence of which we know nothing. All such objections are disposed of and shown fallacious to anyone who studies seriously the esoteric sciences.

But what shall we say of our ferocious opponents, the Kardecists, or the reincarnationists of the French school and the anti-reincarnationists, i.e., most of the Spiritualists of the old school. The fact, that the first believe in rebirth, but in their own crude, unphilosophical way, makes our task the more heavy. They have made up their minds that a man dies, and his "spirit," after a few visits of consolation to the mortals he left behind him, may reincarnate at his own sweet will, in whom and whenever he likes. The Devachanic period of no less than a 1,000, generally 1,500 years, is a vexation of mind and a snare in their sight. They will have nothing of this. No more will the Spiritualists. These object on the highly philosophical ground that "it is simply impossible." Why? Because it is so unpalatable to most of them, especially to those who know themselves to be the personal Avatar, or the reincarnation of some historically great hero or heroine who flourished within the last few centuries (rebirth from, or into, the scums of Whitechapel, being for them out of the question). And "it is so cruel," you see, to tell fond parents that the fancy that a stillborn child, a daughter of theirs, who, they imagine, having been reared in a nursery of Summerland, has now grown up and comes to visit them daily in the family séance-room, is an absurd belief, whether reincarnation be true or not. We must not hurt their feelings by insisting that every child who dies before the age of reason—when only it becomes a responsible creature—reincarnates immediately after its death—since, having had no personal merit or demerit in any of its actions, it can have no claim upon Devachanic reward and bliss. Also that as it is irresponsible till the age of say, seven, the full weight of the Karmic effects generated during its short life falls directly upon those who reared and guided it. They will hear of no such philosophical truths, based on eternal justice and Karmic action. "You hurt our best, our most devotional feelings. Avaunt!" they cry, "we will not accept your teachings."

Eppur si muove! Such arguments remind one of the curious objections to, and denial of, the sphericity of the earth used by some clever Church Fathers of old. "How can the earth, forsooth, be round?" argued the saintly wise-acres—the "venerable Bedes" and the Manichaean Augustines. "Were it so the men below would have to walk with their heads downward, like flies on a ceiling. Worse than all, they could not see the Lord descending in his glory on the day of the second advent!" As these very logical arguments appeared irrefutable, in the early centuries of our era, to Christians, so the profoundly philosophical objections of our friends, the Summerland theorists, appear as plausible in this century of Neo-Theosophy.

And what are your proofs that such series of lives ever take place, or that there is reincarnation at all?—we are asked. We reply: (1) the testimony of every seer, sage and prophet, throughout an endless succession of human cycles; (2) a mass of inferential evidence appealing even to the profane. True, this kind of evidence—although not seldom men are hung on no better than such inferential testimony—is not absolutely reliable. For, as Locke says: "To infer is nothing but by virtue of one proposition, laid down as true, to draw in another as true." Yet, all depends on the nature and strength of that first proposition. The Predestinarians may lay down as true their doctrine of Predestination—that pleasant belief that every human being is pre-assigned by the will of our "Merciful Father in Heaven," to either everlasting Hell-fire, or the "Golden Harp," on the pinion-playing principle. The proposition from which this curious belief is inferred and laid down as true, is based, in the present case, on no better foundation than one of the nightmares of Calvin, who had many. But the fact that his followers count millions of men, does not entitle either the theory of total depravity, or that of predestination, to be called a universal belief. They are still limited to a small portion of mankind, and were never heard of before the day of the French Reformer.

These are pessimistic doctrines born of despair, beliefs artificially engrafted on human nature, and which, therefore, cannot hold good. But who taught mankind about soul transmigration? Belief in successive rebirths of the human Ego throughout the cycles of life in various bodies is a universal belief, a certainty innate in mankind. Even now, when theological dogmas of human origin have stifled and well-nigh destroyed this natural inborn idea from the Christian mind, even now hundreds of the most eminent Western philosophers, authors, artists, poets and deep thinkers still firmly believe in reincarnation. In the words of George Sand, we are:—

> *Cast into this life, as it were into an alembic, where, after a previous existence which we have forgotten, we are condemned to be remade, renewed, tempered by suffering, by strife, by passion, by doubt, by disease, by death. All these evils we endure for our good, for our*

purification, and so to speak, to make us perfect. From age to age, from race to race, we accomplish a tardy progress, tardy but certain, an advance of which, in spite of all the sceptics say, the proofs are manifest.

If all the imperfections of our being and all the woes of our estate drive at discouraging and terrifying us, on the other hand, all the more noble faculties, which have been bestowed on us that we might seek after perfection, do make for our salvation, and deliver us from fear, misery, and even death. Yea, a divine instinct that always grows in light and in strength helps us to comprehend that nothing in the whole world wholly dies, and that we only vanish from the things that lie about us in our earthly life, to reappear among conditions more favourable to our eternal growth in good.

Writes Professor Francis Bowen, as quoted in Reincarnation, a Story of Forgotten Truth*—uttering a great truth:

The doctrine of metempsychosis may almost claim to be a natural or innate belief in the human mind, if we may judge from its wide diffusion among the nations of the Earth and its prevalence throughout the historical ages.

The millions of India, Egypt, China, that have passed away, and the millions of those who believe in reincarnation today—are almost countless. The Jews had the same doctrine; moreover, whether one prays to a personal, or worships in silence an impersonal, deity or a Principle and a Law, it is far more reverential to believe in this doctrine than not. One belief makes us think of "God" or "Law" as a synonym of Justice, giving to poor little man more than one chance for righteous living and for the atoning of sins whether of omission or commission. Our disbelief credits the Unseen Power instead of equity with fiendish cruelty. It makes of it a kind of sidereal Jack the Ripper or Nero doubled with a human monster. If a heathen doctrine honours the Deity and a Christian dishonours it, which should be accepted? And why should one who prefers the former be held as—an infidel?

But the world moves on now and it has always moved, and along with it move the ideas in the heads of the fogies. The question is not whether a fact in nature fits, or not, some special hobby, but whether it is really a fact based on, at least, inferential evidence. We are told by those special hobbyists that it is not. We reply, study the questions you would reject, and try to understand our philosophy, before you dismiss our teachings a priori. Spiritualists complain, and with very good reasons, of men of science who, like Huxley, denounce wholesale their phenomena whilst knowing next to nothing of them. Why do they do likewise, with regard to propositions based on the psychological experiences of thousands of generations of seers and adepts? Do they know anything of the laws of Karma— the great Law of Retribution, that mysterious, yet—in its effects—quite evident and palpable action in Nature, which, sooner or later, brings back every good or bad deed of ours to rebound on us, as the elastic ball, thrown against a wall, rebounds back on the one who throws it? They do not. They believe in a personal God, whom they endow with intelligence, and who rewards and punishes, in their ideas, every action of ours in life. They accept this hybrid deity (finite, because they endow it most unphilosophically with conditioned attributes, while insisting on calling it Infinite and Absolute), regardless of, and blind to, the thousand and one fallacies and contradictions in which the theological teachings concerning that deity involve us. But when offered a consistent, philosophical and quite logical substitute for such an imperfect God, a complete solution of most of the insoluble problems and mysteries in human life—they turn away in idiotic horror. They remain indifferent or opposed to it, only because its name is KARMA instead of Jehovah; and that it is a tenet which emanates from Aryan philosophy—the deepest and profoundest of all the world philosophies—instead of from the Semitic cunning and intellectual jugglery, which has transformed an astronomical symbol into the "one living God of Gods." "We do not want an impersonal Deity," they tell us; "a negative symbol such as 'Non-Being' is incomprehensible to Being." Just so. "The light shineth in darkness; and the darkness comprehended it not" [John i, 5]. Therefore they will talk very glibly of their immortal spirits; and on the same principle that they call a personal God infinite and make of him a gigantic male, so they will address a human phantom as "Spirit"—Colonel Cicero Treacle, or "Spirit" Mrs. Amanda Jellybag, with a vague idea that both are at least sempiternal.

It is useless, therefore, to try and convince such minds. If they are unable or unwilling to study even the broad general idea contained in the term Karma, how can they comprehend the fine distinctions involved in the doctrine of reincarnation, although, as shown by our venerable brother, P. Iyaloo Naidu of Hyderabad, Karma and Reincarnation are, "in reality, the A B C of the Wisdom-Religion." It is very clearly expressed in the January Theosophist: "Karma is the sum total of our acts, both in the present life and in the preceding births." After stating that Karma is of three kinds, he continues:—

> *Sañchita Karma includes human merits and demerits accumulated in the preceding and in all other previous births. That portion of the Sañchita Karma destined to influence human life . . . in the present incarnation is called Prarabdha. The third kind of Karma is the result of the merits or demerits of the present acts. Agami extends over all your words, thoughts, and acts. What you think, what you speak, what you do, as well as whatever results your thoughts, words, and acts produce on yourself, and on those affected by them, fall under the category of the present Karma, which will be sure to sway the balance of your life for good or for evil in your future development [or reincarnation].*

Karma thus, is simply action, a concatenation of causes and effects. That which adjusts each effect to its direct cause; that which guides invisibly and as unerringly these effects to choose, as the field of their operation, the right person in the right place, is what we call Karmic Law. What is it? Shall we call it the hand of providence? We cannot do so, especially in Christian lands, because the term has been connected with, and interpreted theologically as, the foresight and personal design of a personal god; and because in the active laws of Karma—absolute Equity—based on the Universal Harmony, there is neither foresight nor desire; and because again, it is our own actions, thoughts, and deeds which guide that law, instead of being guided by it. "For whatsoever a man soweth, that shall he also reap" [Gal. vi, 7]. It is only a very unphilosophical and illogical theology which can speak in one breath of free will, and grace or damnation being preordained to every human from (?) eternity, as though eternity could have a beginning to start from! But this question would lead us too far into metaphysical disquisitions. Suffice it to say that Karma leads us to rebirth, and that rebirth generates new Karma while working off the old, Sañchita Karma. Both are indissolubly bound up, one in the other. Let us get rid of Karma, if we would get rid of the miseries of rebirths or— REINCARNATION.

To show how the belief in Reincarnation is gaining ground even among the unintuitional Western writers, we quote the following extracts from an Anglo-Indian daily.

[The following passages have been summarized from a longer excerpt appearing in the Allâhâbâd Pioneer.]

METEMPSYCHOSIS

. . . In a missionary production of some pretensions an attempt is seriously made to confute the theory of the "Transmigration of Souls," which betrays an incapacity for metaphysical presentments and an ignorance of psychology that are unfortunate in any person undertaking such a task… The arguments put forward in the paper referred to are worth looking into one by one.

"The first is that metempsychosis 'disregards the evidence of memory.' . . . It so happens that psychologists from Plato downward have called attention to the familiar mental phenomenon in which persons placed, for the first time in their lives, in peculiar circumstances, are suddenly invaded by the conviction that they have gone through the same experience before . . . There is nothing inconsistent with the highest philosophical teaching, or with the moral lessons or the actual experience of Christ; in the occlusions of memory Christ himself, even in adult manhood, under the stress of physical entanglements, sometimes entirely forgot his pre-existent state . . .—why may not any other human nature, not inlaid with an essential divinity, forget for longer or shorter periods its state of pre-existence, if it had one? . . . Theologians may attribute to immaturity of intelligence that apparent unconsciousness of infants, which a keener insight may recognize as the inevitable hiatus between distinct conditions of a human consciousness.

"The second argument is that metempsychosis involves a 'libel on divine justice.' The alleged belief of the Hindus, that suffering in one 'state of being expiates sin in another, which is not essentially unjust, nor a whit less moral than the dogma of inherited or imported sin, may or may not be unfounded; but the first question is—is the atonement of Christ incompatible with transmigration? . . . In what conceivable way can the theory of a man's being a fallen spirit or a risen animal, or both, conflict with what Christ actually said?

"The third argument is that metempsychosis 'is contrary to all sound psychology.' Nine out of ten of the religious teachers who glibly dogmatize in this fashion . . . would be sorely puzzled to explain in what way many of the higher human responsibilities are adjusted between their own psychic and pneumatic natures; and also what becomes of the unity of individual responsibility in the face of this tri-partite allotment.

"The fourth argument against transmigration is that it 'is opposed to sound ethics.' All that any system of sound ethics can demand surely is that personal responsibility shall be attached to every intelligent exercise of individual will . . . Every thinking man must be aware of a growth in his own moral consciousness by which a gulf has intervened between his present and his past: while his personality has survived to identify him, he is aware of distinct stages in his moral nature to which very different degrees of responsibility attach. How does this fact militate against sound ethics?

"The fifth contention against metempsychosis is that 'it is not in accord with science.' . . . But what is there in science that negatives the idea, if it can be sustained by evidence of a natural selection by which if there be any soul at all, the individual soul of a lower organism may pass by stages into higher organisms?"

Karma-Nemesis

By H. P. Blavatsky

Karma-Nemesis is the creator of nations and mortals, but once created, it is they who make of her either a fury or a rewarding Angel. Yea – Wise are they who worship Nemesis [Who dread Karma-Nemesis would be better]-- as the *chorus* tells Prometheus. And as unwise they, who believe that the goddess may be propitiated by whatever sacrifices and prayers, or have her wheel diverted from the path it has once taken. "The triform Fates and ever mindful Furies" are her attributes only on earth, and begotten by ourselves. There is no return from the paths she cycles over; yet those paths are of our own making, for it is we, collectively or individually, who prepare them. Karma-Nemesis is the synonym of PROVIDENCE, minus *design,* goodness, and every other *finite* attribute and qualification, so unphilosophically attributed to the latter. An Occultist or a philosopher will not speak of the goodness or cruelty of Providence; but, identifying it with Karma-Nemesis, he will teach that nevertheless it guards the good and watches over them in this, as in future lives; and that it punishes the evil-doer -- aye, even to his seventh rebirth. So long, in short, as the effect of his having thrown into perturbation even the smallest atom in the Infinite World of harmony, has not been finally readjusted. For the only decree of Karma -- an eternal and immutable decree -- is absolute Harmony in the world of matter as it is in the world of Spirit. It is not, therefore, Karma that rewards or punishes, but it is we, who reward or punish ourselves according to whether we work with, through and along with nature, abiding by the laws on which that Harmony depends, or break them.

Nor would the ways of Karma be inscrutable were men to work in union and harmony, instead of disunion and strife. For our ignorance of those ways -- which one portion of mankind calls the ways of Providence, dark and intricate; while another sees in them the action of blind Fatalism; and a third, simple chance, with neither gods nor devils to guide them -- would surely disappear, if we would but attribute all these to their correct cause. With right knowledge, or at any rate with a confident conviction that our neighbours will no more work to hurt us than we would think of harming them, the two-thirds of the World's evil would vanish into thin air. Were no man to hurt his brother, Karma-Nemesis would have neither cause to work for, nor weapons to act through. It is the constant presence in our midst of every element of strife and opposition, and the division of races, nations, tribes, societies and individuals into Cains and Abels, wolves and lambs, that is the chief cause of the "ways of Providence." We cut these numerous windings in our destinies daily with our own hands, while we imagine that we are pursuing a track on the royal high road of respectability and duty, and then complain of those ways being so intricate and so dark. We stand bewildered before the mystery of our own making, and the riddles of life that *we will not* solve, and then accuse the great Sphinx of devouring us. But verily there is not an accident in our lives, not a misshapen day, or a misfortune, that could not be traced back to our own doings in this or in another life…

This state will last till man's spiritual intuitions are fully opened, which will not happen before we fairly cast off our thick coats of matter; until we begin acting from *within,* instead of ever following impulses from *without;* namely, those produced by our physical senses and gross selfish body. Until then the only palliative to the evils of life is union and harmony -- a Brotherhood IN ACTU, and *altruism not* simply in name. The suppression of one single bad *cause* will suppress not one, but a variety of bad effects. And if a Brotherhood or even a number of Brotherhoods may not be able to prevent nations from occasionally cutting each other's throats -- still unity in thought and action, and philosophical research into the mysteries of being, will always prevent some, while trying to comprehend that which has hitherto remained to them a riddle, from creating additional causes in a world already so full of woe and evil. Knowledge of Karma gives the conviction that if--
...virtue in distress, and vice in triumph Make atheists of mankind. . . --it is only because that mankind has ever shut its eyes to the great truth that man is himself his own saviour as his own destroyer. That he need not accuse Heaven and the gods, Fates and Providence, of the apparent injustice that reigns in the midst of humanity.

Elementary Lessons on Karma

By Annie Besant

Few questions, perhaps, puzzle students more, whether the students be old or young, than that of Karma. What is it? when did it begin? how far does it limit us? are we its servants or its masters? must we fold our hands meekly before it, or struggle vigorously against it? if today grows out of yesterday, and yesterday out of the day before, and so on, backwards and backwards, how can the bad man ever become good? are we not really compelled by an iron necessity, are we not " dumb, driven cattle," who cannot become heroes, whatever poets may say?

We may spend a little time usefully in thinking over these questions and others resembling them, for here, as elsewhere, "a little knowledge is a dangerous thing." Karma is but too often a crippling fetter instead of being, as it ought to be, a strength, a guide, a force, enabling us to act wisely and well. Like all other laws in nature, it binds the ignorant and gives power to the wise.

Here is our first step: Karma is a Law of Nature. We might go further, and say: It is *the* law. For it is everywhere and always — omnipresent, all-pervasive. Other names are given to it in the West, and the names are useful, because they are not surrounded by all the traditions and discussions, which blur the meaning of karma in the East. The Western philosopher calls it *The Law of Causation.* He sees in every happening a double fact — it is both an effect and a cause; it is an effect, for it has a cause; something went before and made this thing to happen; it is also a cause; for it will generate a new happening, another thing will arise from it. As a man is a son of his father, and is also the father of his son; as his father was a son to his own father, and as his son will be a father to his own son in turn, so is it with causes and effects; each event is at once an effect and a cause — an effect of the past, a cause of the future. This observed succession, this invariable relation, is generalized under the term, the law of causation. The human intellect recognizes this law as fundamental, and sees in it the assurance of stability and order as well as of human progress.

We are continually causing effects, unconsciously and consciously. The more we understand our power and nature's conditions, the more can we bring about the effects we desire, and prevent the events we dislike.

The Western scientist calls karma, *The Law of Action and Reaction,* and he also sees it as a fundamental law. *Action and Reaction are equal and opposite,* he says. You push an object; its resistance is its reaction against your push; you fling an elastic ball against a board; it springs back to you with a force proportional to that of the impact. Everywhere in nature he finds this law, and he counts on it with certainty in his manipulations of objects.

In both these Western terms the word *Law* appears. What is a Law — a Law of Nature? It is the statement of an observed succession, of an invariable sequence; it may be put as a formula; wherever A and B are, there C follows. Hence it is a statement of conditions, and the result, which arises from them. It is not a *command;* it does not say "Do this, *or* Do not do this," like a human enactment. It does not say: " You must have A and B, and therefore C; " but rather: " If you want C, you must bring A and B together; if you do not want C, you must take care that A and B do not come together; if you keep A away from B, you will not have C." Hence a law of nature is truly said to be not a compelling but an enabling force; it tells you the conditions, which enable you to produce or avoid a particular thing, and is only compulsory in this sense, that *if* you make the conditions you *must* have the result. Because of this inevitable sequence ignorant people are helpless in the grip of natural laws; they ignorantly produce conditions, and the results hurtle around them, confuse and crush them. As we gain knowledge, we take care as to the conditions we produce, and thus avoid undesirable results.

A law of Nature is said to be inviolable, for this relation between cause and effect cannot be altered. We can disregard natural laws as much as we please, but the law breaks us; we do not break it. If you slip off the top of a building and fall heavily to the ground, you do not break the law of attraction, or gravitation; you disregard it, and your fall proves its truth; a well known formula gives the velocity with which you will strike the ground.

We partly answer, then, our first question, "what is karma?" by the statement: karma is a law of nature of universal validity, called in the West the law of causation, or the law of action and reaction.

The remainder of the answer to the question, "what is karma?" is very closely connected with the second question: "When did karma begin?" A general law of nature cannot be said to have either a beginning, or an ending; wherever there is any manifestation, any universe, any world, there, general laws are also present, inherent in the very nature of things. Attraction of one mass of matter to another cannot be said to *begin;* wherever there are masses of matter, there, attraction is working; gravitation does not *begin,* it is ever manifested where the conditions for its working are present. Hence karma, being, a general Law, is said to be eternal; it is a condition of manifested existence, and wherever existence is manifested, there is karma.

Hence the question: "When did karma begin?" shows a misconception of the very nature of karma; it is a perpetual condition of existence in matter, neither beginning nor ending, but eternal. If the form of the question be modified, and it is asked: "When did the karma of a particular creature begin?" then the answer is: "At the time at which that particular creature came into manifestation." When the unborn, undying Spirit takes to himself a vesture of matter, then he steps into conditions, and comes under the law of karma. His stepping into the conditions begins his particular karma. At first it will be the karma of a mineral, the play upon him of surrounding force and matter, and the reaction from him on his surroundings. These actions and reactions weave the links of his karma, and the chain draws him into one or another type of the vegetable kingdom. In that, as his reaction becomes more complex, the web of karma attaching to him becomes more complicated, and ultimately lifts him into some animal type. In the animal kingdom his increasing sentiency enters into karmic causes, and pains inflicted by him react as pains on him. But the feeling of pain is due to the evolution of the power to feel in him; it is still action and reaction, but where in the mineral these were unaccompanied by feeling, in the animal, feeling results in pleasure and pain: the law is the same; the creature is different, and so the result on the creature is different. As reason develops, another stand is added to the karmic web, and the action in the thought world is added to that in the acting and feeling worlds, and hence another powerful factor is added to the reaction. But once again, the law of action and reaction is working on the same lines.

If the student will constantly bear in mind that karma is action and reaction, and that this works on every plane of nature, works everywhere and always, and is inherent in the nature of things, many of his difficulties will disappear; he will understand that karma begins for him when he descends into the universe of matter, because he has come into the conditions in which karma is perpetually working, and that the reactions on him are exactly equal to his actions, containing more or fewer factors according to those which have gone out from himself.

Another thing that will become clear to him is that the reaction must be of the same nature as the action; hence when a man commits a mistaken act with a good motive, his action is on three planes, the physical, the astral and the mental; the reaction must also be on three planes; the mental reaction will be on his character, which will be improved by the impact of good upon it; the astral reaction will make for him future opportunity of exercising right desire; both these will be good; but the reaction upon the physical plane of the mistaken act will be misfortune to himself. Thus the law works with perfect accuracy and inviolability, and the reaction upon each action follows in unvarying succession.

The idea of rewards and punishments ought not to be allowed to enter into the workings of karmic law. We have results, consequences, but neither rewards nor punishments. Pain is the outcome of wrong activity on any plane, not because anyone inflicts pain upon us as a punishment, but because we have flung ourselves against the law and are bruised against its unyieldingness. The result of virtuous thought or feeling is an increase of the capacity to be virtuous; it is not prosperity, either in this world or another. If we tell a lie, the result is the increased tendency to falsehood, the lowering of our character, and this is an invariable result, not affected by the discovery or otherwise of our falsity by those around us; their want of trust is the reaction from their discovery of our lie; the reaction on us of the increased tendency to falsehood is independent of this secondary result.

"How far does the law of karma limit us?" — such is the question now to be considered, and it falls naturally into two parts: (1) The limiting action of laws of nature, of which karma is one; (2) The limiting action of the special karma, which each one of us has generated in the past.

1. We have already seen that a law of nature is a sequence of conditions, and the conditions among which we find ourselves impose upon us certain limitations. Thus a man cannot fly under ordinary conditions, and if he desires to travel through the air he must supply himself with some apparatus by which he can rise into the air and move therein. The more we know of the natural forces around us, the greater is our freedom of movement amongst them, for we can balance one against the other, neutralizing those which are opposed to any course which we wish to take. If we wish to descend from a tower to the ground by jumping from the top, the conditions are such as to result in the fracture of our bones if we merely jump into the air; but if we arm ourselves with a parachute of sufficient size, we may safely launch ourselves into the air, and float gradually down to the earth. Again, we cannot rise above the atmosphere, and long before reaching its upper regions we should find the air too rare to be respirable; here is a limiting condition; but, on the other hand, we could overcome this limitation by taking with us a supply of respirable air. The power of natural conditions to limit us can very largely be overcome by knowledge, and the larger our knowledge the more freely can we act. Exactly the same is true with regard to the universal conditions called karma; we are limited by them as by the other conditions found in nature, but can neutralize or transcend these to a great extent by knowledge. Hence the enormous importance of studying and understanding the

general karmic conditions, since our freedom is proportionate to our knowledge.

2. Of more pressing and immediate importance is the limiting action of the special karma which each one of us has generated in the past, and an understanding of this is vital for the welfare of our life and the control of our conduct. This understanding will best be gained by a study of the working of karma along the three lines of character, opportunity and circumstances, generated by the three aspects of consciousness — thought, desire, and activity. In the whole of this study it must be remembered that we, who created this karma by our thought, desire and activity in the past, are the same thinking, desiring and acting consciousness in the present; people think too much of karma as reaction on them, and not sufficiently of their own action upon karmic conditions; we modify the outcome of past thinkings by present thinking, of past desires by present desire, of past actings by present acting. Karmic action is not on an inert wall, but on a living consciousness, which reacts on karma and modifies it by that reaction. The passive endurance of karma is seen, and not the active impact upon it; thus a one-sided and inadequate view is taken, and man is paralyzed when he ought to be energizing.

An examination of each of the lines above-mentioned will enable us clearly to see how far karma limits us.

Thought makes character, such is the familiar and true statement. "As a man thinks, so he becomes." The character built up by thought in past lives is born with us in the present life. That we cannot escape, and it is a clear limitation. Let us say that we are born with poor mental abilities; these limit our capacity for acquiring knowledge, and we find ourselves compelled to spend two or three hours in mastering a lesson that our clever neighbor learns in ten minutes. There is a fact, a limitation, which undoubtedly exists. How can we deal with it? For the present we acquiesce in the fact; it is our karma. But, if we know the law, we shall at once begin to exercise our faculties, such as they are, to the full: we shall exert ourselves to the utmost, making up in time what we lack in power. Gradually the limits begin to widen out; thought is exerting its creative power, and our faculties improve under our strenuous cultivation. Accepting the limitation imposed by our poor thinking in the past, we sedulously work at its extension by better thinking now, and thus build up gradually an improved mental equipment for use in the future. Or we may have been born with an irritable temper; contrasting ourselves with a sweet-tempered neighbor, we are keenly conscious of our inferiority; again we feel our karmic limitation. But again we decline to sit down passively within it; we determinedly think patience, until at last we have created it as a faculty, and it becomes our habitual self-expression. Karma may hand on to us our wages for the past in the form of limitations, but karma cannot keep us within that area if we resolutely determine to break them down; within those limits we must begin, but we can change them by the very force which created them.

Desire, makes opportunity: such is the second familiar law. We may have been born clever, but opportunity to show our ability may be lacking; or we may make efforts, which fail of success through *bad luck* rather than through defective workmanship. Clearly we are here hemmed in by a limitation; karma is frustrating our endeavors. Here, again, we must meet the limitation by resistant and persevering effort; we must back up our effort by strong desire, and *will* the success, which eludes our grasp. Gradually we shall create opportunities and conquer our fate, and the limitations will widen out and the obstacles disappear.

Action makes circumstances is the third law. Most difficult of all are the limitations imposed by circumstances; but these also may slowly be changed. The best way is to accept them cheerfully and bravely, adapting ourselves within the limitations from which at first we cannot escape, but keeping up against them a quiet steady pressure, which slowly modifies them. Above all, we should try to increase the happiness of those around us, thinking little of our own, for past selfishness has made present misfortune, and the changing of the cause will bring about a changed effect. Within the present evil live sow the seed of future good, and within the limitations made by the past we create freedom for the future.

We will next consider the bearing on this question of Bhishrna's famous phrase: *Exertion is greater than Destiny.*

Past exertions have made present destiny, present destiny may be changed by fresh exertions. A study of the conditions of such changing will complete our answer to the question: "How far does the law of karma limit us?"

We have seen that *thought makes character*. We look at our own character, and we see that we are deficient in truth, courage and gentleness. How shall we supply this deficiency since it is our karma to be untruthful, timid, and irritable. Thought is our tool for building up what we lack. Every morning we sit down quietly for five minutes and we think about truth. We say to ourselves: "Truth is Brahman; everything rests on truth. In my real Self I am truth, for I am divine. My mind, my body, must express my real Self. Today, I will think truthfully and accurately. I will say nothing untrue. I will do nothing that makes a false impression. O Thou who art Truth, and art my Self, shine out in me as Truth, and help me to be true." Then, during the day, we try to be on our guard against thinking, speaking, or acting untruthfully.

If we exaggerate anything, our morning thought will come up in the mind, and we shall at once feel that we have been untruthful. In such a case, we should deliberately and openly correct the false statement, though we shall feel a little bit ashamed of ourselves in doing so, and this will make us more careful next time. Thus we should go on, day after day, week after week, until we have established a habit of truthfulness in thought, word and deed, and we find, to our delight, that we are instinctively truthful, and the deficiency has vanished, the virtue of truth is ours.

Then we begin, all over again, to build up courage. We think about it in the morning, we practice it during the day. When we feel timid we say to ourselves: "Brahman is fearless, my Self is fearless; my mind and body must be brave." We read about brave people, and dwell on the value of courage. If we see a child or an animal ill-used, we do not slink out of the way, and say: "It is not my business." We go boldly up, and speak gently but firmly to the cruel person, and try to protect the helpless creature he is ill-using. After a time we find that timidity has disappeared, and we have become courageous.

Then we begin again once more to substitute gentleness for irritability; we think on gentleness every morning, we practice it during the day. If a person speaks to us sharply, and our irritable temper starts up all aflame, we force ourselves to be silent, not to answer back; when we can do this without effort, then we begin to answer gently, to soothe the ruffled feelings of the other, until at last we can bear any annoyance without impatience or irritation.

Another very good way of thinking in the morning, is to imagine ourselves perfectly truthful, or perfectly brave, or perfectly gentle. The imagination creates, and we become the model of the virtue, which we have imagined ourselves to be. We think of ourselves as the *very perfect knight*, truthful, brave and gentle, and we become that which we think. By this use of the law of thought we have created new karma, and it has become our karma to be truthful, courageous, gentle. We have established this as our settled character, and we shall be born with it when we return to earth next time. Karma may compel us to bring with us into the world a nature, which is untruthful, timid and irritable, but it cannot compel us to keep that nature. We *can* what we *will*, and karma will give a truthful, brave and gentle nature, if we set going the causes, which produce it;

karma is merely result, and as the one character is the inevitable result of certain causes, so is the other character the equally inevitable result if we choose to set going the appropriate causes.

We have seen that *desire makes opportunity*. We think carefully and quietly of the things which will be really useful to us, choosing the more permanent as against the less permanent, the intellectual and emotional as against the physical. Then we deliberately set ourselves to desire the most desirable objects. We desire them steadily, perseveringly, and we watch for the opportunities, which our desire is making for us, and seize them as they present themselves. But let us remember that the law works unswervingly, and that we shall inevitably find falling into our hands the opportunity we have resolutely created, bringing with it the desired object. If ill-chosen, it will bring disappointment not satisfaction, sorrow not joy. Nature pays over results, indifferent to their nature, and it is for us to choose as we will. Hence the warning: *Take heed how ye pray*.

We have seen also that *action makes circumstances,* and that we lie in beds of our own making. A careful consideration of the relation between our character and our circumstances will teach us how best we may utilize the environment from which we cannot escape. While we diligently try to spread happiness round us, we should take advantage of the conditions to develop qualities we lack. From ill-health we may cull the sweet flowers of cheerfulness and patience; from household cares we may learn tenderness, and develop executive ability; from the drudgery of daily toil we may learn endurance; from anxiety we may evolve fortitude and serenity. The knower of karma turns everything to account and, like a strong and skillful workman, he shapes his future. Karma conditions us, but we are its creators, and in proportion to our knowledge is our control.

The little group of questions remaining is really answered in essence by what has been said, but we may run over certain additional details. " Are we the servants of karma, or its masters? Must we fold our hands meekly before it, or struggle vigorously against it? If today grows out of yesterday, and yesterday out of the day before, and so on, backwards and backwards, how can the bad man ever become good? are we not really compelled by an iron necessity?"

The first question of this group we may pass as already answered: we are partly servants, partly masters — servants by what remains in us of ignorance, masters by all the powers we gain by knowledge. The second question, however, raises an important point. Suppose we find ourselves in the grip of an overwhelming force and any struggle against it is doomed to failure, is there any use in struggling? Every use, as a little thought will show. Let us take a bad physical habit, brought over from the past — drunkenness or sexual sensuality. The man who does not understand karma, says despairingly: "I cannot help it," and he yields without a struggle, and thus weaves another strand into the rope of vice that binds him, making it stronger than before. The man who understands karma says: "It may be that I cannot help it, but I am going to fight against it for as long as I can, even if I have to succumb in the end."

He makes a gallant fight against his enemy; beaten at last by the overwhelming force of his past, he sinks again into the vice; but his noble struggle has broken many strands of that strong rope of evil karma, and when again his foe assails him, the rope will bind him less securely, and he will be able to make a better fight, until — even though it be after many struggles and many defeats — the rope will snap, his limbs will be free, and he will slay his enslaver. When a man has created a vice by evil desire, evil thought, and evil act, he, its creator, can also be its destroyer, by good desire, good thought, and good act. Thread by thread the rope of karma is twisted; thread by thread, the rope of karma may be untwisted; none but man himself creates his destiny, *none else compels*. Take courage, then, all ye who find your present tied and bound by your past; fear not, be of good courage, exert to the very utmost all the strength you have; and you shall inevitably free yourselves, and stand erect as masters where now you crawl as slaves. For law is law, and by the same law by which we bound ourselves shall we now assuredly free ourselves; the law remains the same, and that which in ignorance we wrought by it shall we now through knowledge undo by it, and none can say us nay.

The third question of this group is one which often seems to disturb the mind of the student; must not a vicious man, who continues to live viciously, come back in another life yet more vicious, and so on and on? There are certain counteracting forces, which have to be considered. In the first place unhappiness follows on vice, to some extent in this world, to a great extent in the next. The drunkard, the sensualist, develop a bloated, coarsened body, with shaken nerves and ruined health. How often may such an one be heard to regret his folly, and to declare that if he could live his life over again, he would live it differently. Experience teaches, in spite of our willfulness, and the disregarded law bruises the evildoer. The suffering grows keener on the other side of death, as the scorpion of evil desire stings its nurturer, and the man is forced to recognize that he is living in a world of law, where he may dash himself against the barriers but cannot break them. When he passes from the intermediate world into the heavenly, every seed of good he has within him grows into flower; all that there is of pure and loving in him develops and increases: when the heaven-life is over, the good side of him is strengthened, his faculties are improved. On his return to earth he also brings with him the result of his sad experience as a shrinking from the evil in which before he delighted. The memory of suffering endured, burnt into the soul, has become a cause for avoidance of the evil, which induced it, and thus, by the action of law, is a change brought about in the attitude of the man towards that particular vice. Again, humanity as a whole is slowly carried forward in the great current of evolution, and the evil-doer is carried with it, though he may retard his own progress, almost to the point of stationariness; but this willful setting of a part against the whole, the insolent setting of the individual will against the universal, causes a friction that becomes intolerably painful, and at last ceases by the strong compulsion of this pain. Or again, the evil-doer reads a book, hears a discourse, meets a person, that arouses in him a recognition of the folly of the course he is pursuing, opens his eyes to the suffering he is creating for himself, and stirs his intelligence and his will into an effort to change. Or again, the disapproval of those he loves and honors, the wish to gain affection instead of incurring dislike, these act upon him as a new cause to cease from evil and to do good. Or yet again, the mere fact of his own growth, the unfolding, however slow, of the divine Spirit, which is his deepest Self, inevitably quickens the inborn tendency to good and causes a struggle against evil. Man's tendency is upwards not downwards, and only by doing violence to his own nature can a man grovel in a dust-heap instead of walking with face uplifted to the sun.

"Are *we not really compelled by an iron necessity?"* There is but one necessity, which binds the universe — the loving Will of its Emanator to raise it to perfection and bliss. As God's very Life is the life in His worlds, that Life lifts them ever to higher and fuller expression of Beauty, of Good, of Happiness. Evolution is the essence of that Will, and sooner or later, as the magnetized needle sets itself to the Pole, so must man's will set itself to the divine, whereof it is indeed a part. Man is at strife with himself, and hence the turmoil and the pain. When he sees his lasting happiness, the substance instead of the shadow, then will he be at one with himself and one with Divinity, and enter into the Peace.

www.ingramcontent.com/pod-product-compliance
Lightning Source LLC
LaVergne TN
LVHW041635070426
835507LV00008B/629